CONTROLLING THE SILVER

Controlling the Silver
Poems by Lorna Goodison

UNIVERSITY OF ILLINOIS PRESS
URBANA AND CHICAGO

∞ This book is printed on acid-free paper.

Library of Congress Cataloging-in-Publication Data
Goodison, Lorna.
Controlling the silver : poems / by Lorna Goodison.
p.   cm. — (Illinois poetry series)
ISBN 0-252-02971-2 (cloth: acid-free paper)
ISBN 0-252-07212-X (pbk.: acid-free paper)
I. Title. II. Series.
PR9265.9.G6C66   2004
811'.54—dc22   2004011935

In memory of
Ann Harvey Moran
and Joan Moran

To Myrna and Amlaké

Acknowledgments

Grateful acknowledgment is made to the following, in which some of these poems have appeared or been broadcast.

The Bomb
Commonweal
Calalloo
Wasafiri

BBC Radio
CBC Radio
Radio Mona, University of the West Indies

Special thanks to Lincoln Faller, Linda Gregerson, James Jackson, and Lester Monts at the University of Michigan Ann Arbor. To Swithin Wilmot and Barry Chevannes at the University of the West Indies, Mona Campus. To Tom Lynch and Kate McAll. To Tekla Mekfet for the mother of Jamaican art. To Denis Valentine for the butterflies and the cover. To Ted Chamberlin, and Meg, Geoff, Sarah, and Jeremy. To Liz and Bob Food. To Elaine Melbourne, to my son Miles Goodison-Fearon, and to Paulette and Howard Goodison.

Contents

CONTROLLING THE SILVER

Island Aubade

One bright morning when my work is over,
I will fly away home.
　　　　—Traditional Jamaican

Before day morning, at cockcrow and firstlight,
our island is washed by the sea which has been
cleaning itself down with foamweed and sponge.

Fishermen who toiled all night and caught trash
let down their seines again on the off chance.
The never-get-weary-yet cast off and their nets

will break from abundance. On land, the feeding
trees or kotch-hotels of egrets, bird-bush lodges,
start to empty of perch occupants flown in pursuit

of proverb's worm. The faithful night watchman
will punch the clock and so end dark night's shift.
He earns the right to strike a match, light first fire

and issue out a sheer blue smoke scarf to morning.
She will catch and tie up her hair with this token,
gunman and thief slip and slide home with long bags.

And the farmer turns in the sleep that is sweet,
a laboring man sleep that, he'll flex his wrists
in practice for machete wielding; and the woman

will give suckle to a drowsing infant. In the field,
the low of cows in need of milking ministrations.
The jalousies of the choir mistress, who sleeps alone,

open as she raises a revival hymn over the yard
to hail the coming of our Lady of Second Chance,
the Mother of Morning who invites all visitors.

❁

Come drink this cup of Blue Mountain coffee
stirred with a brown suede stick of cinnamon.
Just say no thanks, what you need is bush tea.

Pumpkin seeds parched, steeped in enamel pot
with kept-secret, fitted lid, so no steam escapes
before you raise its doctor-vapor to your face.

Thank source, she will insist, for the mysterious way
spirit debones from troubled flesh, easing you
from sickbed across entrenched ice and tundra

up the seven thousand feet peak of Blue Mountains.
Startover is where Mother Morning lives. By leaven
of struggle-up mantra, return Shulamite to Xamayca.

Morning has become my mother, bringer of curing
bush tea. She is now mother to the whole island,
grandmother to Miles, mountain born, who thought

'Maw'nin' was a lady. "Show her to me" said my son,
and we pointed him to a rose dawn over our village.
Above our house was Blue Mountain Inn, the Queen

of England dined there, we did too, till hurricane
raised high the roof. She comes bringing frangipani
and jasmine commingling in a clay jar of terra cotta,

cloth cotta on her head coiled to bear, asking where
we want these bride-ivory flowers dew-drenched
from wedding nights. Set them on the Singer machine

by the door of a concrete-nog cottage where wrote
the penkeeper of Enfield. Chalk-white walls scripted
with calligraphy of ivy, acid-wash, slate roof porous

in parts, board latches to doors and windows gaped
wide so as to allow loquacious choirs of gospelling
redthroat birds to chorus in the brick floor kitchen,

where I stood over a gas stove and stirred, porridge
for my boychild, for his dog, cornmeal and beef bones.
Stirred, till we arranged ourselves as migrating birds.

Emulate the fit fruit that mother of morning brings, mark
June plum's defensive seed, so deep the purple skin
concealing the milk-flesh of most private starapple

(which Miles consumed only in twos). She always has
the same greeting, our lady of second chance morning.
Hear her: "my children, come in like the new moon."

If we encounter turn-back northers and land after noon,
she will be pleased to fix us second breakfasts of cooked
food. Sweet potatoes, medallions struck from yellow yams,

unfertilized ground provisions we'll eat seated under
poinciana trees, which drip petals, like scotch bonnet
peppers, capsicum benediction on our second breakfast.

Don't shake hands with the wicked, eat greens, abase
and abound. After this, no one you'll meet is a stranger,
she'll say, and give you a mesh fan of flexible ferns.

For this Jamaica sunhot is hell on your skin, burnt raw
by radium. Going to bathe in the family river cousin,
we need to go back to where our people come from.

3

Over the Guinea Grass Piece

Fly the shutters and dun-winged sparrows beat in.
Leave ripe fruit and Demerara sugar
out on counter; let them drill through rind skin
and clear plastic, till sweet-mouthed they perch
beside this new sheaf and sing. Wedding weed
trails from the kitchen windowsill, garlands
for attendant bridesmaids. Pink corallila
embroiders the green hedgerow of bush bush.
A matched pair of brown and white milch cows graze,
nurse egrets needle flanks free of leech ticks.
A brown calf draws down its mother's warm milk,
the poinciana shivers blood issue
of petals over the guinea grass piece.
To the west the Caribbean sea, Atlantic
waters to the East.
We always said we'd go back together.
You who loved a sick joke, here is one:
we are crossing the Tropic of Cancer.

Dear Cousin

i

We might not reach in time to de-ice you
into renew. You lie in the foothills

of Calgary and I'd like to be able
to tell you that the azure harbor ahead

is the horseshoe of Lucea Bay, but those
white horses run too fierce.

You have the eye, from the foothills you can
discern the washed bones of many million

drowned on the Atlantic side,
where long-meter waves hexameter swell:

Wild horse, mounted militia, martial law
search and destroy, thundering buffalo,
bull bucker, overseer, guineagogue,
badlove-takelife waves, gathering brute force
to draw you under, come girl, wash your heart,
with heart-rinse of machete-split coconut.

ii

They packed you in ice early up north
where you plied your wordsmith's trade,
rubbing the salve of convince on dry tongues
which became then sure and swift of speech.

Your own tongue aches from tip to root;
you want to assuage it with water coconut,
for killer crab and that low grey lizard
beneath the water jar have harmed you.

When at age seven our two eyes made four,
you were my first cousin who taught me
how a river named by our generations
was benign, would not harm, but pull and haul,

bank to bank safety. You said to me, sit there
on the grave stones town girl, sit and learn
how to discern between one good duppy
and a bad one. Under the damp, dirt cellar

of the Harvey house we exhumed porcelain
bowl shards, buttons of bone, blank-stare dolls
with decayed bodies, and nacred spoons we used
as earth-moving tools for finding Harvey roots.

Excavating

the long line of David and Margaret,
disinterring evidence of the stillborn
who did not draw breath at begetting time.

Which begins with Nana Frances Duhaney of Guinea
and William Henry Harvey of England, who wed
and begat Tom, Fanny, Mary and David
Harvey, he who wed Margaret, progeny

of Leanna Sinclair also of Guinea and George O'Brian
Wilson of Ireland. This is how we come to come from
the long-lived line of David and Margaret,
who begat Cleodine, Howard, Edmund,

Alberta, Flavius, Edmund, Rose, Doris
and Ann. And I am from Doris, and Joan
she was from Ann, but it was like we were
daughters of one woman. Come in cousin

from the cold: there are times a one has to
seek succor under own vine and fig leaf.
Let us look now to the rock and quarry
out of which our generations were hewed.

Ode to the Watchman

As we exit from the old city before day
we sight the night watchman at his post,

evidence of his vigilance against nocturnal
furies red in his eyeballs. He did not bow

though, no, not him, it is right to thank him.
All praise to you O beneficent watchman

for keeping guard over us while we slept,
blessed be your eyelids which did not blink

even once in solidarity with those lowered
shutters, window blinds and jalousies.

You remained awake, ever alert, armed,
with only your night-stick, rod, and staff,

your aged, cross mongrel dog rampant
at your side, even as the smoke pennant

blown from your rough-cut filterless
hand-rolled cigarettes flew out full staff.

For pushing against that grease-stained
tarpaulin of despair and not allowing it

to befoul us during our needed night rest.
For keeping at bay restless rolling calves,

trampling down from those sleep hills,
busted old rusty chains rattling to shake

the firm resolve of small hearts, thanks
watchie for keeping them from breaking

and entering our little children's dreams.
And now kind watchman go home to rest,

you who did not seize and beat the beloved
as she roamed the streets, composing the Song

of Solomon. Go home now good watchman.
The last hot rush of caffeine pins that pricked

your blood awake has been rained from your
thermos flask, your bread-back of night lunch

cast upon the keep-up fire in your belly. Cease
the anti-lullaby you keen to maintain wake,

the sun is here to take your place.

Our Ancestral Dwellings

Columned cotton trees are our ancestral dwellings.
Beneath them stand the departed who missed
the return voyage on redemption's longboats.

Cravers of salt, gravalitious warriors enlisted
in world wars of must-have; stirred-up ones
with unfinished business who cannot lie quiet.

Necessary guides, who without warning occupy
the skins of fervent women, commandeering
prayers to sound earthquake and storm warnings.

Undelivered orphan children seeking rebirth,
engorged navel strings in need of clean-cut,
for only then can they die and come in again.

These are ones congregated at cotton tree root,
some offering themselves for hire as if alive.
Others limbo there till moved by hosts to depart.

We have no business here. Drive past.

Recalling the Fourteen Hour Drive from Kingston to Lucea, 1953

At least fourteen pit stops or maybe more
for engine fires to be extinguished,
to pee in the bush, then to Old Harbour
for Arawak bammy and crisp fry fish.
We leave come sun up, taking the two-lane
highway, risking our necks over Junction
Road. Chant psalms aloud, as we careen down
and around Mount Diablo's hairpin bends.
Then more stops to throw up and seal off chests
with newspaper. One hundred and ten miles
past cane fields, citrus groves, banana walks,
tall palms this island was then home to. You
lifted up your eyes to them, you small child
pressed in the back seat between big people.

The Wandering Jew and the Arab Merchant on the Island of Allspice

Along the road we passed the wandering Jew
in his dark suit, his cart piled with dry goods.
Further along, we sighted the Arab merchant,
his wares rising from his back in a camel hump.

Attar of roses, good for your noses, come to you
from me and Moses. Buy your perfume pressed
from those fragrant rose blossoms of Lebanon.
All the way along the Damascus road, the Jew

has come to sell his things to the freed Africans.
The Arab came following the long spice route
to this island of Allspice. Shalom and Salaam
becomes 'Sallo' on the tongues of the Africans.

They were known those days to find themselves,
the Arab and the Jew, in the same free village,
on the same day, peddling their similar wares.
And in the village square they would sit at noon

under the broad shade of old Lignum Vitae trees
and break bread together, unbraid Challah, share
aish or Syrian bread. Aish, ancient name for both
bread and humanity. They'd sit, eat and remark

how some hard-pay Africans do not like to part
with silver, and how they both dread the walk
through cockpit country. The Arab gave the Jew
a chip from the ka'ba to protect him in the valley

of the shadow. The Jew gave the Arab an amulet
shaped like Moses' tablet. To the Africans, they sell
Bibles, then all bless Father Abraham, before taking
to hill and gully roads across this island of Allspice.

Passing the Grace Vessels of Calabash

Our foreparents carved on
(lest they forget) maps, totems
symbols and secret names,

creating art when some
would claim we existed
in beast state.

Every negro in slavery days
had their own
hand-engraved calabash.

So they'd drink water from
grace vessels, their lips
kissing lines of maps

leading back to Africa,
to villages where relatives
waited for years

before they destroyed
the cooking pots
of the ones who crossed.

So Who Was the Mother of Jamaican Art?

She was the first nameless woman who created
images of her children sold away from her.
She suspended those wood babies from a rope
round her neck, before she ate she fed them,
touched bits of pounded yam and plantains
to sealed lips; always urged them to sip water.
She carved them of heartwood, teeth and nails
her first tools, later she wielded a blunt blade.
Her spit cleaned face and limbs, the pitch oil
of her skin burnished. When the woodworms
bored into their bellies, she warmed castor oil;
they purged. She learned her art by breaking
hard rockstones. She did not sign her work.

Jah The Baptist

FOR THE RASTAFARI ELDERS

Children call the fruits of locust trees, stinking
toe. Are they what John the Baptist fed on?

In those Bible stories our mothers read to us,
John the Baptist was dread righteous Rastaman,

trodding wild in the desert, feeding on honey
and locusts, "herbs for my wine, honey for my strong drink."

Balancing acrid with sweet of wild bees, he invoked
brimstone, lightning and fire on generations of vipers.

Flee, he warned, from Babylonian standards. Play not
by the rules of their game, for they detest the dark

of your skin, the thick of your lips, the wool of your hair.
Strive not to imitate Babylon, become your own man and woman.

Before he baptized with the waters of clear insight,
hard-case words of locust musk kicked off his tongue.

Poison Crab

That bunch of corroded keys
dropped in your lap, now hangs
deadweight on your days.

In morphine sleep you dream
by the bottle-torch moonlight
of village children, owners
of the roads in crab season.

Crack backs underfoot
sever limb from limb
snap those antenna eyes
scoop articulated parts

into long bags hauled home
to boiling pot. They stiffen
before yielding up flake-flesh
to scourge of hot pepper,

bow broad forehead
to strike-down of hammer.
But always there are ones
that bite back and do not let go,

till thunder roll.

Let Us Now Praise Famous Women

No, begin this praisesong again,
for our foremothers obscure,
canonize them right and left.

Since oncologists read
crab tracks in your cells,
you summon female spirit warriors

like cousin Fool-Fool Rose
who rose from being
village idiot to world class praise singer

because she practiced
legendary Xamaycan hospitality
and offered up her cup
to a stranger wanting water.

Fool-Fool Rose is Leaving Labor-in-Vain Savannah

Grass cultivation upon roof top
hot sun striking it down to chaff,
Rose bundling with strong effort
scorched fodder fit for Jackass.

Rose securing sinkhole in river
with rock salt and rose quartz,
to find favor with headmaster
inspecting her morning tea sugar.

Sign on sign and she did not heed,
returning to shut-bosom mountain
spite river's mouth spitting weeds.
Open lands with not enough room

for her to raise a modest Rose tattoo.
Soothsayers in their suits well-pressed
prophesying Rose-death from fatigue,
expecting a legacy of marrow secrets

scrolled soft-tubed in yielding bones.
A quiet stranger came empty handed
to the well; Fool-Fool Rose offered up
her cup, in thanks he uttered key words

that turned her from housetop agriculture,
and locked off her ambition to bottom
and dam a river hole. Farewell/hosanna,
Fool-Fool Rose is leaving Labor-in-Vain Savannah.

Rainstorm is Weeping: An Arawak Folk Tale Revisited

The weeping Rainstorm from our reading book
bore strong resemblance to Aunt Cleodine.
Her full head of hair whipping up great shocks
of black rain clouds, her tall body wedged
between heaven and earth's birth passage,
and rainfall her eye-water on storm days.
She craved power, Rainstorm, for here it said
in the reading book she trained her hard gaze
at those installed on clouds, and made her way
to exalted places to sweep them out by force.
Sadly, she got stuck between sky and earth,
the reason she weeps, and why flood rains fall
Octobers and most Mays. And when she rails,
she invokes the levelling hurricanes.

Aunt Alberta

Amazing how Aunt Alberta was named by an act
of sheer prescience after a Province of Canada. Alberta
born 1903 on the island of Jamaica,

one Easter morning cracked an egg and sighted a ship
becalmed between yolk and albumen. Taking a hint,
she boarded a steamer and sailed

faraway from life in a sun-lit green Jamaican village
founded by her grandfather into a city of ice storms.
No lingua franca but the tongue

of Quebecois, and unaccustomed hard labor in Mont Royal.
She lived in service, taking orders; a saint remitting
money and care-parcels for an entire village.

Photographs show her dolorous in snow banks, solitary
in deep sylvan glades of photo studios, till at aged forty-
four she married one Geoffrey Seal,

a Barbadian, himself stone-faced in service, first and only
man to uncover her loveliness. It came unexpected,
Aunt Alberta's late luck, in the form

of a tender companion who wore her wool scarves
like prayer shawls, holy her barely-scented handkerchiefs.
He slept, telling her pearls like a rosary.

Aunt Rose

Our favorite photograph shows her in a blush-pink
Parisian spring suit. Observe the soft felt cloche,
the high-heeled shoes, tendrils of suede straps
x-ing across insteps, kissing her long narrow feet.

Damask Rose, too gorgeous, reduced sincere men
to silence. They'd end up drumming nervous digits
on taut throat-skins, attempting to tap out wooing
messages, appropriate toasts to the Rose of Sharon.

Even in Montreal, where gilded French women
would go, exalted by haute couture, she'd cause
Quebecois men to groan "mon dieu" and plunge off
street cars calling "comment s'appelle Mam'selle?"

Beauty concentrated, top to base note she trailed.
A human pomander, the very particles and waves
of her roseate self would scent odorless atoms.
Her essence permeating skin, blood, bones, flesh,

she drew in breath and blew out rosewater scent.
Fragrance-deficient ones begged caresses from her
scented hands which in the end became coated
with attar of Roses. Attar yes, Rose knew burnings,

but the fair Rose of Jericho, never wanting to speak
of such scorchings, would press down her torched
voicebox, scarred and keloid with beauty burns,
to the last releasing rose scents, but no sounds.

The Burden Bearer

My sister Carmen's hair uncombed
sprouts like fronds of the palm tree.
When the fits take her, she convulses
like a palm tree in hurricane season.

"I am the burden bearer," she moans
as she spasms, foams and falls, assuming
position of family scapegoat come to bear
for all, one hard bitter-gall life of battering.

The one with sores no blue-stone cures.
The one with scorch blister of the brain.
She who is designated to carry the weight
of our people's communal sin burden.

My sister does not bear silent, she stirs
word-salads of poems, badwords, psalms.
She's learned by heart most of King James's
Bible, she wields its language as weapon.

Yea verily the Bible says honor thy mother
and thy father, but parents provoke ye not
your children to wrath! She curses my mother
for the fall from a vehicle while carrying her.

For the deep cut to her brain which festers
and erupts, testing our house's foundation.
Job-like she wants answers to hard questions.
Out of all my parents' nine children, why her?

Travelling with Photographs of Our Generations Flanking St. Christopher on the Dashboard

We stop at the seaside and recall how our Arawak
ancestors fished for the deep-sea gold snapper,
which rose goggle-eyed at swift haul from bottom
up to air element.

It opened its mouth, a few gold coins fell out.
They paid Columbus' taxes with that, and that
is how, we their heirs, come to speak freely
in tongues:

(Scatter all cling-cling off a mi red wall.)

We inheritors of fishbone which builds floating ribs,
providing us with calcium for dissolve into sleep.
We the eaters of fishhead which gave us brains,
developed fish eyes to see over curved distances.

We perceive how the Coratoe shines, rooted gold
on sloped hillside. See the Shameweed chastened,
hold down its head and weep.

Observe red and yellow pride of Barbados
(not as tall as it thinks it is) preen and mark
boundaries with dildo macca (domestic barb wire).

By this sea that our ancestors walked on
their barefeet pierced by Jerusalem thorns.

Hosay

After warm rains the West Indian ebony lifts its arms
and salaams blossoms. Stop the car and join the Hosay.

On their indentureship he steered them straight
to the West Indies: these Indians come in bond to Cane.

Hosay, Hosein, East Indians delight in offering praises
to their Spirit Guide, the son-in-law of the Prophet.

He their one kind overseer in the mud-sop of rice fields,
Hosein himself would weed rice and root turmeric.

Benevolent master he bestowed on them great gifts;
so the African Jamaicans would one day come to believe

"Indians get talent to drive truck and catch fish."

He their present Patron Saint revisited Jesus' miracles
and charmed the fresh fish of la mar into wide nets.

Instructor Hosein is who taught them to steer
the prosperity path away from cutdown razor grass.

In thanks each year they construct for him a marvellous
multi-colored house, and hosay across the Savannah.

Creation Story: Why Our Island is Shaped Like a Turtle

On the Shell gas station map, Jamaica,
big-up and large over broad Caribbean sea.

The pin head of our village turns up and pricks
your finger so a drop of blood spots Harvey River.

We're really on the map now you say, then wonder
why our island is shaped like a swimming turtle.

A possible explanation:

Swimming turtle smitten with hot sun
paddles up from water bottom in search
of light become her love object.

Turtle call is ska beat, turtle tail licks
riddim, tail of turtle, nine miles long
forms sea-side of Negril.

Turtle implores Creator, leave me here.
I choose to fall from heaven under
the water to be with hotsun.

So creator strikes turtle with stick,
her shell cracks, in rush big rivers,
hills and high mountains swell up.

Turtle strikes bargain with Creator
to remain above water, housing Taino,
Europe, Africa, India, Asia and China

just to be with sun, and tell the world
that Jah Mek Ya, so Jah said, Yah.

These Three Butterflies and One Bird
We Interpret As Signs

i

Historis Odius Odius

Leave earth Nymphalid,
soar and stay bourne within
spirit breath, doctor breeze's
reviving, bearing currents.

Do not pitch now or pause
to malinger over sugar mill's
whatleft, trickledown leak,
or lick blackstrap molasses.

Avoid caprice breezeblow
or any old batterbruise fruit.
To feast on over-fermentation
makes you white-rum drunken.

Keep the pace, this trajectory
will take you to fat-leaved
feeding trees, far from poison pin
and trap net, fly on, hard fi dead.

ii

Tiger Swallowtails

When fully grown, Tiger Swallowtails
have swift roaming flight patterns.
Their unprepossessing caterpillars

are not much to look at, resembling
droppings of dull-plumaged birds.
But despite their crap appearance
they persist in arching themselves
to feed from chalice-petalled tulips,
till one day they lift out of pupa state,
flashing their V-shaped markings
and at wing-tip, topaz tiger's eyes.

iii

Urania

Truth is, you are really moth's blood relative.
But unlike your Cuban cousins, you do not flock
to the seaside with escape rafts, or show any
predilection whatsoever for sea grape,
cocoloba.

And on account of your formal appearance,
dark velvet dress with transverse bands
of ruddy gold paved with powdered gems,
some say you are swallowtailed butterfly
which you are not.

For often in winter before tourists arrive
you're found taking sun under mangroves,
confounding lepidopterists claiming to be
your superiors and most learned colleagues.
So they believe.

And then the Bird Banana Katy

These green gold hands
checked by tallyman
hefted by broad-back
gave you your name, Katy
bird, go eat of them.

Last night we stopped
at a hotel for dinner;
a white-jacket waiter
stripped one naked,
doused it in cane liquor,
and set it on fire. Katy
it blazed like a cane field.

Behind every bush
lurked an African
determined to return
to Igboland or Guinea.
Shadows danced macabre
on terrace walls.

Hibiscus oozed
blood wounds
crickets chafed
hind legs
beat wings
riot riddims.

Surf pounded
like wardrums.

Burnt sugar
seared the air

red-jacket waiters marched,
marched like militia.

Today we'll just
drive on and chew
on the rose-heart
of the good guava.
Fly over there Katy,
and feed on your banana.

The Geovangelist

In that obsidian rock wall
behind our ancestral home
seashells are embedded.

They were excavated by
the geologer evangelist come
to our village to Uncle Flavius.

The foreigner had received news
of uncle's migrations from church
to church in pilgrim effort

to behold his Creator's face
closeup from all angles. He came
bearing news of a new religion.

Upon his arrival in our village
the geovangelist ran to the rock
and casting himself down

spent one entire day prostrate
on mourning ground before
plunging metal into stone.

Chips like black coral flew.
"Molluscs, there are seashells
in this ancient rock's face,

people this rock was once
under the sea. I believe it may be
rock of the lost continent Atlantis."

That was his theory, which as far
as we know was never proven.

Don C and the Goldman Posse

We drive past Discovery Bay
and conjecture how Columbus may
have heard of this rumor about
Jamaica once being part of Atlantis.

Don C and the goldman posse
arrived by leaky caravelle taxi,
and barely make it to the beach,
and as dem reach so, dem start
with the hold down and take way.

Buy out the bar with counterfeit.
Eat off the bammy and roast fish.
Turn round and wipe-out Arawak
with pillage, plunder, and disease.

Hours beat, the Don C posse leave
because no gold was really on here,
except for that let off by the sunset
into the sea, which makes small boys
leap over white limestone cliffs for it.

Back To Where We Come From

We are approaching
the archway of courtly bamboo,
the family river wets the stems
of rooted reed instruments.
Touched to lips of the wind
they pipe, "this long time
gal me never see you."

We had hoped that we could enter again
into the stone and wood House of Harvey
and sit. That relatives might bring cooling,
four water jelly coconuts, two each.
That we'd light the Home Sweet Home lamps
with their deep froth border of glass lace,
that after we catch up ourselves, we'd leaf
through sepia snap shots and then reread
early lessons from the Royal Primer.
That we'd sit down on family tombs,
then go to sleep in our grandparents room
in their four poster bed till morning came
and we'd consult with the river's keeper.
But instead we are confronted with this.

O Pirates Yes They Rob I

Capturer cousins in a great land grab
have claimed the ancestral Harvey house
and levelled it. A rickety banana walk
crowds the tombs. On a lean wash line
garments washed with the envy-stain
of green bananas, flap like dingy ghosts.

A stranger woman, capturer cousin's wife,
has tied up a ram goat where grandmother
Margaret cultivated prize roses she watered
with green tea. We are disinherited children,
you and I, who stand in the road and weep.

Wife of the capturer never reveals herself
but sends from behind the stained scrim
of the knock-knee clothesline a small boy
in a khaki costume, addressing us directly.
He speaks, "she say to ask you, who you be?"

And we be the great-granddaughters
of the founders of Harvey River, village
and river, where once was a kind of Eden,
with captured Africa retained on small
hillside plots. Where our grandfather
David gave freely of his own inheritance
to raise up a branch of the Church
of England, and our aunts in Montreal
dispatched by Royal Mail candlesticks,

patten and chalice of brass, French lace,
altar cloths, censor and thurifying
frankincense to ascend each Sunday
as prayers over this village; even while
the goatskins of Ogun hammered the bassline
and homesick Africans moaned.

The gods of England and Africa
worshipped cheek by jowl.

Who we be? Fertile some of us; but some
have loins hard as the black rock behind
what was our house, which is now just shell-
evidence of an era when our people owned
a village and welcomed visiting cricket teams,
and hosted those pleasant Sunday evenings,
and were village scribes and lawyers
who wrote letters, read newspapers and defended
the defenseless against the savage laws of the land.

On St. Patrick's day it was great-grandfather
George O'Brian Wilson who crooned Irish
airs that fell and took root as casuarinas
beneath which he caused our great-grand-
mother Leanna to fall, wanting as he did
then to ingest her Guinea essence as it rose
in a light ellipse from her griot throat. But
she swallowed hard and retained her story
which I was brought here to tell. Who we be?

Long-lived as a rule, except once every fifty
years one of us has to die young, so the rest
of us can live long, and all we want is to sit
down in peace upon our people's gravestones.

Tombstones

i

Here lies the body of David Harvey,
Father of our Mothers, village lawyer
lover of literature, farmer and scribe,
Catechist of the Church of England.
Born of African mother and English
father, we bring water to wash his
grave, root up stray weeds and bless
his ivory bones for the compassionate
marrow soft in them, powdered now
to mineral ash, fallowing this bearing
earth, giving of himself to the last.

ii

And this is where the last remains
of Margaret Wilson-Harvey, wife
of David Harvey, were laid to rest.
Daughter of a griot Guinea woman
and Irish father; her humor dark
as porter, as her mother's onyx skin.
She who cautioned all her children,
hard life is a chance game; prepare
to play any underhand that it deals.
Her plain tomb rejects all worthless
weeds, parasite vines do not thrive
here, to the end no one overruled her.

iii

The lamb's wool of Uncle Howard's
head was shorn; same head opened
by a stone. Behold red water grass
about his tomb, testament to rush
of blood let from him, admitting
furnace fever, then death itself in.
He being the first one to die young.

Where the Flora of Our Village Came from

Credit the Spaniards with introducing sugar cane
plus the hypocrite machete that cuts both ways:
Columbus encouraged Arawak to grasp the blade
of his keen sword even as he smiled a greeting.

Pindar nut, Cherimoya and Alamanda—stowaways
from South America. Ipanema girl Bougainvillea,
since she land, has been in one extra Miss Jamaica
contest with Poinciana, Madagascar hottie hottie.

For mangoes and pungent ginger, thank East Indies.
For jackfruit and the high-strung chattering pod
wind-activated, christened by someone acquainted
with carry-go-bring-come, the woman's tongue.

Courtly bowing Bamboo came calling via Hispaniola.
Mother of chocolate cocoa, is Polynesian Gauguin girl.
The silk pulp of Chinese hibiscus, crushed, blacks shoes,
and zen-like bleeds to ink for penniless school children.

Coffee, kola, ackee, yams, okra, plantain, guinea grass,
tamarind seeds and herbs of language to flavor English;
those germinated under our tongues and were cultured
within our intestines during the time of forced crossings.

By the Light of a Jamaican Moon

A tongue-bath of moon.
And your countenance
is glazed.

This compelling force
draws you to it,
inclines your face
and silvers it with kisses.

Catch is, your face is turned.

Your desire
for moonlife
raised like sea level.

You tidal pool,
and dryland dwellers
wake and find you
watersource in their midst.

You are not sure
how you reached,
but you let them drink.

You can read by the light
of a Jamaican moon, so we read.

Lessons Learned from the Royal Primer

FOR VELMA POLLARD

Taught us how Bombo lived in the Congo
in a round grass hut. Bombo was the boy
who sported a white cloth about his loins,
causing one of our linguists to conjecture
that perhaps Bombo's rough garment gave
the name to one of Jamaica's curse-cloths.

Now we were never told exactly what
that little boy Bombo was doing, except
just dwelling as a dark Congolese native
in his round-domed grass ancestral hut,
supported by a thorny center pole. But
what the Royal Primer forgot to tell us

was this. It seemed that it was the king
of Belgium who gave strict instructions
to his soldiers to cleanly chop off both
the little boy Bombo's hands, on account
of the fact that balls of rubber cultivated
by Bombo were deemed too lightweight
and not enough for the needs of Leopold.

Hirfa of Egypt

Guess who I met up with in Egypt? Hirfa,
in a souk, over a glass of mint tea.
She informed me through an interpreter
she did not know that she had been featured
with a stink camel in Royal Primer
and that they'd made her look ridiculous.
(That book made Giza's pyramids seem small.)
Hirfa said that she was no Camel Girl,
vowed she'd wear no lattice-eyed burqua.
That she'd study under Hapshepsut,
iconoclast, female Pharoah and Queen.
Hirfa is now revisioning herself,
with a lion's body crouched to leap
and with a woman's head uplifted.

What of Tuktoo the Little Eskimo?

Whose father sawed round holes in the ice
and dropped his rawhide line baited
with bloody gut from previous catch
and hauled large pearl-scaled fish up,
then dipped icy fish flesh in cool seal oil
and filleting its fishmeat with a bone knife
fed it to each of his many children in turn.
Fish being brain food made Tuktoo wise,
he became a cinematographer and recorded
the Inuit's true ways through fish-eye lens,
an epic named Atanarjuat the fast runner.

Arctic, Antarctic, Atlantic, Pacific, Indian Ocean

The world's waters rolled into a chant, we learned
the oceans by rote and song. Arctic began with 'a'
drawnout and soon the crowded class would rock
back and forth on wooden benches packed close.
With a low moan, is how Arctic started. Along came
an ant, and Arctic became Antarctic, body of water
that left us cold, until we reached Atlantic. Then
we suffered sea change, and would call out across
the currents of hot air, our small bodies borrowed
by the long drowned; Atlantic, as if wooden pegs
were forced between our lips; Atlantic, as teacher's
strap whipped the rows on, to learn this lesson:
Arctic, Antarctic, Atlantic, Pacific and then Indian.

Louis Galdy of the World's Once Wickedest City

He (Galdy) set up as a merchant in a modest way, but soon found his fingers in
many pies—merchandise, shipping ventures, produce dealing, the slave trade. . . .
—Clinton V. Black

As blond, black-skinned sailor pickney scrambled
down back alleys warbling "you done
dead already" Galdy would just shamble
through the ruined town of Port Royal stunned.
In the wake of the fall of Christendom's
wickedest domain, some power spared
him to tell the tale. What had he seen down
when earth engorged him? Inferno maybe.
Cut-throat, scurvy sea dogs, doused in white rum,
become torch men in sea of molten goldpiece.
Bawling badmen waving letters of marque
and asientos, Galdy just went quiet.
After earth swallowed then spat him to sea,
he ceased the buy and sell of human beings.

Remittance Man

Arriving with a band of thespians,
he took up with and married a native
and promised not to return to England.
For this promise made, his family gave
him upon the first of each month, D.V.,
a stirling sum by H. M. Royal Mail.
In time he became the theatre critic
writing on the efforts of the natives,
likening them to characters known on
the boards of England. Thus Louise Bennett
was Puckish, Sagwa Bennett, Falstafian.
A few remarkable presentations
were declared to be worthy of Burbidge.
Then there came a day that the natives said
they would like to comment upon themselves.
Taking umbrage, he turned his pen on them.

Black Like This?

To the girl in the great house who cried
as her nurse bathed her
"If you touch me I might turn black"

some questions:

Black as decay signalling
seek cure, cut-out, abandon?
Black like trick-light of raven
revealing what in you is broken?

Jet like johncrow absorbing
collective curse and rejection,
swallowing carrion, keeping
the corruptible kingdom clean?

Black as night's courtly love
for light, keeping her at days end
under the wideness of his tent,
delivering her virgin to the world?

Black like deep shelter-holes
where stars go to expire, hiding
the lost-cause of their falling?

Black like that you mean?

Pleasant Sunday Evenings

Our grandfather David, reader of high
English verses, hosted pleasant Sunday
evenings where the villagers recited
local and literary works; poems
that they grafted into hybrid flowers,
poor man's orchid and milk-like coffee rose.
New world horticulture, cultured from slips
some eloquent oilymouth let fall so,
as he or she worked over sweet John Keats,
spraying him with African mouth water.
So you would get lyrics sounding like this:
"woe add, two a night, tin gale, buy junkets."
John Keats, friend of those with not long to live,
patron saint of pleasant Sunday evenings.

Passing the Empty Playground

Hush over the play field,
children fielding cricket balls
drop catches, abandon gully and slip.

He's been spotted across the boundary,
walking barefoot over fields of police macca,
the razor blade of his awful business
stained rust from his latest cut-out
of some innocent's heart.

Beware the Blackheart Man, children.

No righteous rastaman this one.

Run little ones, scatter,
recite our father, our father
all the way home.
Sign the sign of the cross
over target hearts, match abandoned.

Think we'd recognize him again
when we saw him.

What the Witnesses Saw When They Entered the Balm Yard

(From an account in the *Star* newspaper)

Your honor, when we the witnesses entered
we saw her seated in a brimming bath tub
aboil with green bush. In her right hand
she clenched an upraised sword, between her teeth
was clamped a silver coin with a lion stamped on it.
She bite it like a bullet. Bite it till the lion
was all but decapitated.

And that man there,
the thickset one with the eyes like pitch, he was
balming her. He balmed her for pain of belly;
but he used nightshade instead of cerasee.
He balmed her for quick guaranteed success.
He balmed her against enemies—some of whom
were friends. Then he balmed her for himself.

This River Named by Our Great-Grandfather

is the first water boiled and cooled you sipped.
This water that soaked infant birdseye napkin
and rinsed poplin chemise, is the water source
that christened, confirmed, and baptized you.

Under anaesthetic you wrenched off the mask
and slipped under, your clear skin tinged green,
your dark eyes, fish-eyed. You could always suffer
change and stay under. That was your water gift.

Every child born in this village received skills
from the river's guardian. Take for example
your sister Myrna. She's the appointed rescuer
of souls in danger of going under. She's the one

trained to stay the frantic mind's frenzied waves
so the storm-tossed can tread water. She stands
on bank and shore at night, alert to grave signs
of distress; a light streams from her forehead.

Myrna labored to direct you on to dry land.
You remained under unconscious, collecting
such specimens as you'd need to receive treatment
from River Mumma. Wedge of hard brown soap

our Grandmother Nana let fall as she scrubbed
her big tall husband's drill shirt and trousers.
The wedding ring of that village girl whose man
went off to Cuba and forgot to return. An I.O.U

of old debt owed, inscribed on parchment
with silver point, coated with powdered bones
and sealed in an hermetic scroll which had to be
opened and paid to that man from the land of Cush.

River Mumma

She sits with her back to us, her teased hair
is now bleached platinum. She has affixed
paillettes of rhinestones and sequins over
her shimmering scaled skin (here we have
a perfect example of how to gild a lily).

Please tell the River Mumma we are here,
outside the doors of her underwater clinic.
We say this to nurse souls rolling bandages
and grinding medicine bluestone in mortars.

Though we see how her hairstyle has changed
(it used to dip so evenly in regular waves),
and we see her lips are stained parrot-fish red
and her hobble skirt is bling-bling iridescent,

we still bring her this serious crab bite case
who is in need of her specialist treatment
(hair of dog; water cure for bite of crab),
for maybe River Mumma medicine can cure her.

We bring a wedge of brown soap for cleansing,
a lost wedding ring found, to make payment.
Details of one fraudulent agreement we seek
to bleed indelible ink from, Mumma please come.

All the while the drowned souls drape bandages
in long white strips across the clinic's entrance.
Deaf to us, the drowned ones pound bluestone
in mortar pestles. We are not acknowledged.

The River Mumma Wants Out

You can't hear? Everything here is changing.
The bullrushes on the river banks now want
to be palms in the Kings's garden. (What king?)

The river is ostriching into the sand.
Is that not obvious? the nurse souls ask.
You can't take a hint? You can't read a sign?

Mumma no longer wants to be guardian
of our waters. She wants to be Big Mumma,
dancehall queen of the greater Caribbean.

She no longer wants to dispense clean water
to baptize and cleanse (at least not gratis).
She does not give a damn about polluted

Kingston Harbour. She must expose her fish
torso, rock the dance fans, go on tour overseas,
go clubbing with P. Diddy, experience snow,

shop in those underground multiplex malls,
spending her strong dollars. Go away, she will
not be seeing you, for you have no insurance.

The Wisdom of Cousin Fool-Fool Rose

Two middle-aged mermaids who got soaked,
we re-enter the village running the gauntlet
of the relatives calling: Morning cousin this,
Morning cousin that. Morning cousin from foreign.
You hear the news, cousin from across the water?
Our dear cousin Fool-Fool Rose is on-dying.

In her one room, prostrate on her single bed,
the red gold and green headscarf worn off
for the first time in must be fifty years;
her locks like wool serpents scroll Aramaic
script across the tablet of her white pillow.

We ask her:

Cousin Fool-Fool Rose,
how do you bear the spite of death,
old hige, bitch, long in claw and tooth,
rip and chewing flesh to dry bone?

She smiles and points to a calabash gourd
netted. A red, green and gold crocheted reticule.

I and I sight that bag there? When death fling pain
the I open I mouth wide and swallow, then spit.
When it full, the I fling the bag over I right shoulder.

Such wisdom the I learned when the I sight up
the quiet stranger by the well. The gift
of I cup, the pure intentions of I heart
was enough to set I on the path to wisdom.

The I departed from Labour-in-Vain Savannah,
and went to dwell instead on the road to Heartease,
among the likeminded who defend peace,
who labor only to mend the tear-up world.

For the record, the I was never a one who walked
ten steps behind any Kingman. The I never sight up
to become downtrodden. The I became instead
handmaid of wisdom of the order of Grandy Nanny.

Look through the window and sight that cloud,
floating cotton mattress or a level-vibes carpet,
as how I and I feel to call it. The I tie the mouth of this bag
and then the I mount upon that flying carpet cloud

with this bag full of beating, and the I ride.
I and I and I am kin, through the line of Guinea woman.
I and I and I come from generations of horsewoman.
How I and I bear death's slings and arrows? I and I ride.

The I can sight up from the way I and I look soak-up
that I and I penetrate below, seeking for an answer
from River Mumma. But the old order is passing
and things are not the same beneath the river.

But why I and I go there for? No true wisdom seeker
should ever depend on that sometimeish spirit,
that uncivil servant of Babylon who should retire.
Verily the Kingdom has not removed, it is still within.
To get the wisdom the I seek, I and I must cleanse.

Wash face, hands and feet, rinse out hard-ears, and pass
clean wet hand (benediction) over the crown of the head
thus reopening the mole (fontanelle). I and I will become

once again as an innocent. Then get flat on the ground
and beg the Most High, entreat the Most High for help.

The cleansing of the feet, face, hands and crown,
the thorough washing out of the channel of audition,
is a vital move, for I and I like that obedient little youth
to hear and say "speak Lord, for thy servant heareth."

The bag is full, the cloud is here, the I must mount the flying carpet
which lifts the I out of the range of death stabs aimed at the I flesh.
The I destination is Heartease; but to reach there, the I must ride.

In the Field of Broken Pots

Water goblet, bitter cup or monkey jar.
Know that each of us has been part of one
of the above; and that in time we're bound
to become broken down into small shards.

In a vision that night River Mumma came
and grudgingly dispensed to you a pill of clay.
You swallowed it, then lay down and joined
the vast deposits of like returned to ground.

You said: that was my answer, but I don't want
to go yet. You said:

In a West African village, on the day I depart,
women will gather my clay pots in the field
where the vessels of all departed are smashed
so that the dead are never equal to the living.

The plain terra cotta rounded cooking pot
patterned with my daughter's palm print,
the goblet I glazed with crushed gems, then
sketched on with thorns, will all be broken.

Only weaver birds, and ants who sip raindrops
from shards, will ever drink again from my pots.

O weaver birds and ants who drink of raindrops
promise you will come as guests to sip of my pots.

But I May Be Reborn As Keke

Keke, piece of broken clay pot
used now as base to start new pot,
culture of clay that went to fire
and returned to function as talisman,
keystone, sure-fire foundation
of new water jar; made the age-old
walk around way. Coiling the rolls
to make cool water hold in smooth
cheeked monkey jar. Keke, old heart
of used pot, cast back on wood fire
but flame proof this time, sure guide
of new jar, shard of which will become
in time, keke, most kneaded clay.

At Harmony Hall We Buy an Egyptian Blue Cecil Baugh Mug

Black blue as a Toureg he surfaced
from his Nile baptism: then came fever.
Parched, he returns and swallows
Portland's Blue Hole, licks the sheen
off leaping marlins and fires kiln
with heart-wood of the Blue Mahoe.

Blue stone of Borax: wound cauterizer.
White body: ancestor's bleached bones.
Cornwall stone: rock of the west.
Clay of China: Orient transported.
Carbon Oxide rendered it dense
or glaze would slip transparent.
True jewel, not faience. An Holy
Blue came through our master potter.

Change If You Must Just Change Slow

We will crouch down then in a red earth
hollow, press our lips close to the heart
of this deep Cockpit Country and call out
please don't change or change if you must
just change slow. Old countryman riding
jackass, big woman watering the dry peas,
fat cow, and mawga dog, one-room dwelling
with intricate carved lace fretwork eaves.
Heaped yam hills, garlands of green vines,
cockades of bamboo on crown of the hillside.
Little bit a country village place or woodland
name of Content, Wire Fence, Stetin, Allsides,
far from domain of gunman and town strife.
Country we leave from to go and make life.

All the Way to Kingston We Recall Urban Legends

And was Long George, AKA Sea Cow,
really the island's tallest man?
And did he legally take as wife
Tiny, the shortest of all women,
when a fly-by-night two-ring circus
with a mangy one-eyed mawga lion
pitched tent—admission one shilling—
to see tear-arse clown and unsteady
trapeze act in Kingston Race course?

Remember how after the circus came,
our old dog 'Bullet' went astray? Boys
in the neighbourhood claimed our canine
had been sold to the circus for lion-meat.
We the children wept a bit, but truth was
we didn't miss Bullet; the dog was known
for biting even small hands that fed him.

Whatever Became of MaMud?

She the Michelin tyre woman
wearing a Makonde mask face.
No Kingstonian doubted MaMud
was the most corpulent of women;
MaMud, landed proprietress
of downtown Kingston tenements,
brothels, rum bars, and fishing boats.

MaMud, whose stomach housed
whole schools of mullets swimming
upstream in gastric tides of coconut oil.
Hot pepper buoys bobbed in her throat.
Prescient wheatfields of dumplings,
ten seeded acres of Rangoon rice,
sprouted just to stay her appetite.

The mud squelch between bare toes
going "MaMud, MaMud, the yield
of this field is to feed our MaMud,
O great mother of perpetual eating."

The Yard Man: An Election Poem

When bullet wood trees bear,
the whole yard dreads fallout
from lethal yellow stone fruit.

And the yard man will press
the steel blade of a machete
to the trunk, in effort to control

its furious firing. He will dash
coarse salt at its roots to cut
the boil of leaves, try slashing

the bark so it will bleed itself
to stillness. And yet it will shoot
until the groundcover is acrid

coffin color, the branches dry
bones. Under the leaves it lives,
poverty's turned-down image:

blind, naked, one hand behind,
one before. The yard's first Busha
was overseer who could afford

to cultivate poverty's lean image.
But this yard man says since we
are already poor in spirit, fire for it.

Controlling the Silver

Her silver-money necklace and bracelets
made agreement with the wind that went
like this: if she rode upon her gray mule,
seabreeze would kiss and coins protest, creole music.

Silver coinage; England minted, soldered
into flexible chains then freely draped
about the neck and wrists of our Guinea
great grandmother: controller of silver.

Let us praise now market women: higglers,
who maintain our solid, hidden economy
in soft money banks between full breasts.
Gold next; now these women control silver.

In those Sunday markets across the island
the sold Africans would gather, ostensibly
to sell their ground provisions, cultivated
at the end of long days in service to cane.

In what-left hours, they transformed rock
hillsides to bearing ground under the shine
eye moon, which is why ground provisions
gleam when tumpa knives cut them open.

Let us praise now artisans and craftworkers,
builders of Empire. Skilled ones who raised
up temples of marble. Masons and carpenters
constructing suffering into stone and fretwork.

Dovetailers of joints denied benefit of all union.
Hail O basket weavers, potters, calabash carvers,
seamstresses of garments stitched from ripped-
off ends of regulation oznaburg; skilled recyclers

of missus' old clothes. Bush doctors, gatherers
of curing herbs. Hawkers of vengeful potions,
Myalists, Pocomania and Revival practitioners.
New World Christians remaking massa's religion.

Praise to those gathered in common markets,
redemption grounds where Africans swapped
blood secrets, kept spirit, passed on information
about insurrections, and bought and sold silver.

So the silversmiths developed a brisk trade
in bracelets and guard rings; the thrifty bury it
to dig up one day and buy freedom. The silver
likes market culture, stays there, does not leave.

Deep shut-pans of silver lie buried at tree root.
On moonless nights you may walk by coin-light,
if your good foot happens to kick loose a lid
a source of pent-up shining will be released.

Crocus bags of silver still banked beneath
banana trash mattress (we should look for it).
Draw of silver passing from hand to hand
in a susu/partner (you must pay the banker).

One day the coinage runs so hot it runs out.
The Governor has to be told that if he dies
that night with his two eyes wide open, there
might be no silver coins to keep them closed.

Not a threepence, a sixpence, not one florin.
No metal-alloyed between the stirling notes.
Not even a lion-pon-it shilling to connect
one pound to guinea, absent all the silver,

except for that revolving around the body
of our women like Jupiter's multiple moons,
plunging between black mountains of bosom
into drawstring vaults of calico threadbags.

These women accustomed to Guinea gold,
these people late of Benin, now control silver.
Enough to buy land, even to lend to massa,
every coin a cocoa, filling up their baskets.

Full baskets of Redemption Ground Market.
Bob Marley's muse followed him home
from there, when he went as country boy
to buy raw cow's milk, and two yard fowls.

By day a market, by night hallowed ground.
The workplace of productive angel bands
and anointed spirit guides with real power
in the blood to wheel you free from crosses.

Wheel you till take-set spirits stagger back.
"I was a smoker, I was a drinker, a backslider,
God see and know I was a thief, till the Holy
Spirit collar me, and spin me like Ezekiel's wheel."

Praise to the power of our Guinea woman great-
grandmother, higgler with pencil in her tiehead
to cancel old debts, seamstress with the scissors
in her right hand who will cut for us fit pattern.

Nana who can balm you clean in five bush bath.
Big woman, who can afford to pay Peter a shutpan
of silver as indulgence for your soul. Mercy agent
seated astride her gray mule, come to ride you home.

Old Blue Nun

Wolf-grey mist snarls over Long Mountain range.
Cloud cover, or bush fire struck from flint and stone,
and no trees stir.

We live all summer underwater, duck the headlines,
dive deep when neighborhood grapevines bear
spilled-blood fruit, avoid especially TV news,

and take refuge in FM radio. But today that warns
of hurricane. Wonder, would it be cowardly to return
to the north before the banshee waterwind blows

as we speed past the convent of Stella Maris nuns,
where old blue sister once invited me in, said kneel
bow, pray, make three wishes.

That made me wonder, what kind of a nun she was,
of what order, Sisters of our blessed fairy godmother?
And if saints travel with the brothers Grimm?

Kneel, pray and make three wishes. My wish as I kneel
is, I pray you will rise from that white bed in Calgary
to pass clean through the storm's eye.

Making Life

Jah never run no wire fence
—Bob Marley

The cherry afterglow of Negril spring break,
sunset rays knit into his tam from the gold
ball dropped behind Rick's cafe,

my student oversteps a gray snowbank
on Liberty to ask me "Lorna, how can you
live in exile?"

Because it would take too long to tell
how I left because my Jamaica was like
a faceman lover

with too many other women he was seeing
on the side and I might have just died
waiting for him

to finally get round to doing right by me.
But that is too long a story, so I wander
and wonder instead:

is it because we came from a continent
why we can't settle on our islands?

Did our recrossing begin with deportation
of maroons to Liberia via Nova Scotia?

Are we all trying to work our way back
to Africa? For soon as we fought free

we the West Indians picked up foot
and set out over wide waters, to Cuba

and Panama, anywhere in the Americas.
And we never call ourselves exiles.

We see our sojournings as "making life."
So after world wars when they wanted

souls to bury dead and raise near-dead,
they called us in as duppy conquerors.

But when the job was done, they then
tried to exorcise our task force,

but we remained, took their brickbats
and became Blackbrits and Jamericans.

I first came north to paint pictures, but
maybe I wanted firsthand acquaintance

with the fanciful places named in songs.
Isle of Joy, the song said Manhattan was.

I'm from island in the sun, I had to come
and my sweetheart poetry joined me.

Not really exiled you see; just making life.

Your Ice Art, Michigan

Across the wide snow-primed canvas you paint
with vegetable, mineral, water and oil medium,

there are skeletal groves of charcoal stick trees,
put-to-bed fields and high rise totems which

accept salt sacrifice thrown at their feet. Except
for blocks of primary color barns, your palette

is toned down with frost tempera. When you draw
ribbons of skim-milk rivers, you loop and loop them

till they connect with Superior's waters, then burst
into true blue in exuberant recognition of source.

Admiration for your perfect composition laid down.
Bands of roads run straight and across, intersect

then part. So effective your ice art that some days
I have no need to favor green. Still, I remain,

expectant witness to your up-from-tomb spring.

Broadview

FOR JOHN EDWARD

Take the red streetcar that stops at Broadview
you will come to a sealed lane named Brydale
by walking along wool weaver's avenue.
On the corner in a tall rented place
with stained-glass cathedral windows live now
two people whose lives add up to over
a century. Two who took a late chance
to mend and solder their divided selves
into strong binding two-toned interlace.
Torches carried became welding flames
for trying days; briar ways they came
through acres long untended. At ease then,
scythe rank choke weed, lower the nightshades,
sweet thyme take root in perfumed herb garden.

Missing the Goat

Here we create new rituals, fill a crystal
goblet with dried redbud drawn sorrel
purchased late this December snow day
from Chinese Trini in Kensington Market.

À votre santé with drink so wine-alike,
gingered, spiced, hybridized wassail cup
the jewel juice of Xamaycan hospitality
raised to this our first joined Christmas.

For the feast we had planned a portion
of curried goat accompanying a turkey.
But the host of yardies peopling this city
came before us, got all goat and have gone.

Even the papershod, halal-butchered ones
plunging from Greek meat shop windows,
Esther Williams in a dive on the Danforth,
are now bought, sold and gone everyone.

Does mass exodus of sacrificial goats mean
the first-comers will have days of plenty
and we late sleepers mere fowl flesh? No,
in season of wine on the lees and marrowfat,

we'll feast then on curried some-other-flesh.
Raise our crystal goblets garnet with sorrel
to Advent arrivals and small constellations
of now beneficent stars over our night rest.

Spirit Catcher

The big Indian holds council on the mercy seat
by the doors of the church we tried to join.

We tried, my love and I, to return to the religion
of John Donne and George Herbert.

But the minister was from the order of Greene's
whisky priest (for God's sake, his wife took
communion in an old T-shirt and shorts).

Twenty below and big Indian gathers his band
on the hard bench occupied by the Danforth's
most destitute.

Take this drunkalready; asleep, wrapped, a roman
candle swaddled in frayed remnant of discarded
sanctuary carpet.

Prodigal girl; deaf to entreaties of father bearing
white box of deli food, as he implores return O
daughter to your Rosedale room.

But she elects to stay with Big Indian hawking
spirit catchers, crafted from leather, beads,
feathers, whalebone, glass.

Dazzle-hoops through which orphan souls leap
into Great Spirit's arms.

The Crying Philosopher and the Laughing Philosopher

Inspired by a Rembrandt Etching

The Crying Philosopher

For 99 days this city has been covered with snow.
Today will make 100 days since the streets
have been under deep cover. All snowfall metaphors
are officially exhausted. No seraph's eiderdown
torn, no celestial beer-head foam from Valhalla
mead mug. This is bully-boy and bitch-spite snow
in attack mode and treacherous. In origin pristine,
at last state become soiled, lowlife, gutter fodder.

The Laughing Philosopher

All is for tomb-rending time when the white garden
revives, full color. This chill blanket shields bulbs
and forsythia. Rhododendrons, wheat and azaleas
need downtime under ice cover. Chaste monk's hood,
indigo, iris, and provence lavender require annual dye
of blue ice water. Dead then awake, ground water table
risen so high the faithful walking, come April, on water.

All Souls Day

How to explain Kumina drum sounds
resounding through these cold rooms?
From what sky did a gold disc drop
this percussing cymbal in my teacup?

More music now, here's a reed wind
which pipes alto and animates March
trees. Waterfowl on the pond become
canards who honk in duck-deep chorus.

And no matter how my used-heart tries
to settle like a cabouchon-cut stone
in the weighted crown of an aging liege,
it ska ska skas instead, licks one drop

like the wingslaps of duck, oblivious.
All day I seem to have company,
sitting down by myself to eat, I sense
that someone already spread this table,

prepared this meal then graced it for me.

Hard Food

Decked in her finery, Doris would transport
every specie of provender. Opting to jettison
her own garments when the scales registered
outrage, scandalized, horrendous overweight.
Not one finger of green banana surrendered.

She journeyed to see her sisters Rose and Ann,
her suitcases fat with the food of their Hanover
childhood. In advance, she'd hunt and gather
Lucea, white and yellow yams, sweet potatoes,
and cassava, green, Bombay and Julie mangoes.

Sheated in the obituary pages of newspapers,
they landed ripe, fit for sucked-dry endings.
So they read, they ate, sure of finding at least
one soul known to them in the death columns.
"See a Duhaney dead here, she must be related

to grandmother Nana." Bliss is a ripe Julie mango.
"Wear Pimento grains in your socks for heat."
"Mama where you get that kind of foolishness?"
She never said. My mother, possessor of esoteric
information, boss of things strange and arcane,

packed sugar cane next to aloes and tamarind.
Foil-wrapped escoveitched fish like silver slippers.
"When I land, I'll cook for them. We will feast
whole night till morning." On my way to Calgary
with a bag of hard food, mother I've become you.

Breadfruit Thoughts

"When you come again," Joan said, "bring a breadfruit."
But I brought instead these breadfruit thoughts.

When he delivered the bounty, did the masses
hail him as hero?
That hardcase sea captain who elected to water
breadfruit seedlings
rather than give his crew fresh water to drink?
Tough it out Bly,
through foul weather and Christian mutiny.
Did they say, God bless you Breadfruit Bly,
for sake a you, yellow-heart thrives,
it's flesh fired, assumes texture of bread buttered?
Did Jamaicans beat goat-skin for phenomenon
of starch-of-life on branches?
Was breadfruit scorned, thought to be slop for hogs,
till hungry bite like yaws and caused Jamaicans
to consume breadfruit roast and boil?
For bread brought, did Bly receive inside-out
roast breadfruit heart?
Just a few breadfruit thoughts.

Rites

Past the Drumheller badlands and Sylvan Lake
the shaman came at dawn by way of Red Deer
and made for the Foothills, where he rattled bones
in a bladder pouch, built fire in a smudge pot
and washed her in sweet grass smoke, to no avail.

And if special rights could have been transferred
for me to become a Blackfoot medicine woman
skilled in the use of puff balls to stem hemorrhage
and the administration of mind-clearing bullberries
beaten off branches just after the fall frost, had I been

made honorary Blood or Piegan dancer in a jingle dress
trimmed with copper tinkling cones to sound scatter
for crabs, I would have doctored and danced. Instead
I stood by the window and watched her go the way
of great female buffaloes at Head-Smashed-In-Jump,

those matriarchal leaders of herds with wild bangs
of coarse black hair and dowager humps she and I
dreaded we'd inherit. 'We thought we had more time,'
reads a caption in an exhibition on Plains Indians
at the Glenbow Museum. We thought we had more time.

Carnevale

i

"Oh shut off the Schubert," Joan said to the nurse,
sounds so vinegar and cool cannot help me now.

The Indian woman one bed over, mantras David Rudder
"and we aint finish, we aint finish, we aint finish yet."

Bring me, my cousin said, that music

from an angel wrestler with long shank stretched
when Africa held his head and Europe his feet
so that Isis could deep kiss him.

Bring to my bed that Trini Psalmist King
to chant me into my too soon tomb.

ii

Twenty-five years ago when the Mighty Invaders paused
in sprinkling half-light to hammer out Unchained Melody
for the badjohns of Port of Spain who had not made bail,

it was Pan Aubade by the Royal Jail: light rain.

Here, a confession: that was the hydra year my ambition
was to flee poetry to become a nun, wife, or flag woman.
Ten years from that dawn, my friend Bernard powdered
down from six feet four into a foot-high alabaster urn.

King David,
King David Rudder

Ras Mass is a High Mas, we play it for Jah Jah.

Play now at soothsayer:

This year when mighty invaders pass, Bernard
will arise and walk out to the other world's iron gates
to escort my cousin in. Dr. Tom Yew, take care of Joan.

Aunt Ann

Ann Rebecca, bird of paradise,
is that you grey-owl watchful
among clay plots of Mount Royal
Cemetery where your washbelly
last child resides, sent off by her
own girl in a drizzle of red roses?

Ann Rebecca, are you dark-eyed
from presiding over new grave?
In watch and pray mode do you
pilgrim go, through Côte de Neiges'
streets each night trumpeting
down stone walls and iron gates
to enter and protect your charge
confined now to a narrow bed?

Does morning find you unseeing
by windows, dear Ann Rebecca?
Accept, aunt, a jar of dead-sea salts.
Anoint it under heart, massage
its brine savor over your chest.
Caress the place you first detected
her infant heart-beat, there she is,
connected. The lovely are passing.

The Liberator Speaks

Down the avenue of Ficus trees
with overlapping braided roots,
late-rising blackbirds carry news
from eaves of cool blue buildings
housing ministries, to the sea side.

They fly over bands of school girls
in sheer white stockings, who sing
as lush memorial wreathes are laid
at the stone bust of Benito Juarez.

And there to the right of Benito
stands Simon Bolivar, The Liberator.
Ascetic, watchful from extended vigil,
listening for Spain's imperial knock
come to lead him away blindfolded.

Ah, the sweet levitation of Spanish.
Language held, clipped, then loosed
so that those Habaneros who claim
its custody, can question the tongue
of these other Spaniards of San Juan.

Simon Bolivar would sometimes
turn to the nubile Jamaican girl,
daily bearer of his midday meal
wrapped in a clean linen cloth,
breast of dove. Turn and bid her

listen as he spoke his liberation
plans in strong creolized Castilian.
The liberator confiding fervently
aired out detailed secret schemes
to a young still-spirit African girl

silent as obsidian. When he stopped
she then rose, adjusted her skirts,
collected her empty mahogany tray
and departed. Plans for the liberation
of the Americas bound in her braids.

Palm Roses

"My name is Juan"
he informs tourists, and draws
a long spear from his quiver
of green leaves, then flashes
a blade and shaves the leaf
into sprays of palm roses.

"These last forever"
Juan promises, unlike the bruise
lesions on his body set to go
when he lays down his AIDs
cross on slag stones like lapis
along the Calles of St. Sebastien.

"Buy your Salvation Roses"
just a six-dollar indulgence
for three. Juan kneels down
as he grows them from air,
leaf and blade, then he creates
five fishes for his daily bread.

At the Keswick Museum

Amidst the packhorse bells, cockfighting spurs,
the glass walls of stuffed birds, and a giant set
of cordierate impregnated stones which sound
to create an early form of xylophone, it stands.

The wooden chest you are asked to handle
with care, for it houses the 500–year-old cat.
Its concave eye sockets still scoop darkness.

In those days darkness was on the whole land:
take for example in the parish of Lampligh
in 1658, the following deaths were recorded.

Three frightened to death by fairies.
Four perished from being bewitched.
One old woman put to death for maybe
bewitching the four just mentioned.
One poor soul led to unfortunate end
by a will o' the wisp carrying her wide.

In addition, educated people in Lampligh
claimed their domiciles were inhabited
by bogles, spirits and dobbies (duppies).
A dobby or duppy it seems, was or is
an household spirit which can get mean
and vicious if not hospitably received.

So there in the Pastoral Lake district
the good people found it was necessary
to root frightspirit rowan trees by gates,

and to place oddly shaped, waterworn stones
(preferably those with a single eye-hole
representing the all-seeing adder) atop walls.

Eye of adders to ward off witches, bogeys,
dobbies, all categories of malevolent spirits,
including nightmares, which were steeds
ridden by witches like the one put to death
for taking the life those four souls. So when
they took her life, her cat gave up his ninth.
That's it there petrified in that wooden chest.
Cross yourself and just back away from it.

Bam Chi Chi La La: London, 1969

i

Calm as a Coromantyn warrior baring his chest
to the branding iron, this man was standing outside
a corner Lyons in January, wearing a thin floral shirt.
One helluvabitch cold tore at the hibiscus over his heart.
So he unbuttoned button after button until almost
barechested, he stood calm as a coromantyn warrior
giving it up dry-eyed to the white hot branding iron.

ii

In Jamaica she was a teacher. Here, she is charwoman
at night in the West End. She eats a cold midnight meal
carried from home and is careful to expunge her spice
trail with Dettol. She sings "Jerusalem" to herself and
recites the Romantic poets as she mops hallways and
scours toilets, dreaming the while of her retirement
mansion in Mandeville she is building brick by brick.

Half Moon Bay

At big sea site, real fishermen went deep.
Some settled on the salt cays; fishermen
and badmen, Jimmy Cliff as Rhygin
in Harder They Come, missing getaway boat.

At Harbour View near the Harbour Head
beach we the children battled squadrons
of slabba jellyfish; boys peed on own feet
to dislodge seaeggs' hypodermic needles.

Half Moon Bay: big sea outside open door
my love like the salmon in spawn time
has come home this year to be reborn.
Sea lions roam along this open waterfront,

sharp-face seals puncture waterskin,
slap and lick surface, somersault deep.
New-hatched family of geese promenade,
the young black hawk straddles the air.

Arriving at the Airport Once Called Idlewild

Pilgrims practicing strict worship. The captured
in darkness vessels, stowaways who limbo
under those quota bars, come to these shores.

Lorna, Althea, my friends my sisters; one-heart
for putting me up in your walk-up apartments
on your good Samaritan's fold-out couches.

How the great city showed me man-made beauty,
skyscrapers solid as blue and green mountains,
towers now replaced by beams of blue lights.

I am sorry for your loss.

One hundred newspapers to Jamaica's then one,
one thousand radio stations to our two.
I was charged by the waves of human energy
conducted through every borough of New York.
I visioned my father, revived by it, come through
cement portals of a funeral home in Regio Park.

Reviving wave wash.

Apollo Double Bill

Those parrot fish men in pimp regalia,
red light red to bottom of the barrel blue,
issued forth from whale-sized cadillacs
sliding soles of dyed alligator skin shoes
across the slick pavements of One Hundred
and Twenty-Fifth Street and Lennox Avenue.

Whatever you do
don't ever make eye contact with a New Yorker

because they might be packing.

"Now," said he, "you wouldn't just happen to be
some of them girls who when singers come on
start screaming and shouting now would you?"
Enquiring man clad in head-to-foot red,
with gold teeth ample to light up stage,
wants to know.

So my friends and I, all full-of-mouth,
fine-feathered, turned out for hot fun
in the summertime, stare him in the eye
and backanswer, "what's that to you?"
"Cause if you are," he says, unlocking
his red rib cage to release a steel shape
that shifted to his hand,

"I'll be forced to take my forty-five and silence you."

Not a peep from us as we sat, wings dropped.
Till we slipped to the fowl roost where unchecked
whoops and whistles, pillow-fight feathers flew.
This was after all the "Sock It To Me Summer"
double bill with Junior Walker and his All Stars
plus the sweet-boy Smokey Robinson. What could
any young girl in Summertime do but scream?

For all the music, New York: Hugh Masekela at the Village Gate,
Arthur Prysock in Central Park, James Brown at the Apollo,
Les McCann at the Bottom Line. In nineteen hundred and sixty
eight inside Sam Goodys on Broadway, John Coltrane blew
and split open the bark of my young green Tamarind heart.

Guernica

On the third day I went with Seymour Leichman
to the Museum of Modern Art, there to see Picasso's
Guernica, and the woman bearing a lit lamp burst
through the casement at the upper left-hand corner
of the canvas; the disemboweled horse screamed.
Swift sleight of hand; Basque woman dropped fire
in the niche Coltrane split with the lip of his horn.

Turpentine top notes, base notes of linseed oil; scent
of painters' studios can cause salt to wash my eyes.
It was originally my ambition (that is why I'd come)
to become a maker of most marvellous pictures.

So I apprenticed for a time in the studio of Brachman,
and then under master painter Jacob Lawrence. Great man.
Don't look to right or left, just do the work, do the work.
Slip past those petty guards at the Metropolitan's gates
who'll seek to dispatch you on their fool's errands and
do the work good, Jacob said, just do, and do the work.

Catch me running with that city rhythm. Up in the morning,
take bus to the train, take train to West Fifty-Seventh Street
to the Art Students League. After classes take the A train
to filing job on Wall Street. File, then take train to Greenwich
Village, there to cashier at the Rugoff's Fifth Avenue Cinema
between Twelfth and Thirteenth. So train and paint and train

and file and train and cashier and so see the second half
of a movie. I saw the body of work of Akira Kurosawa
in parts. Swords of Seven Samurai, claw-foot of Throne
of Blood, round about midnight, rode the night train home.

Winter vespers in a Village church, I offered up prayers
to St. Jude, invoking as litany a Beatles song. Home came
the boys in body bags to be replaced with fresh live ones.
I am that I am, and I am beauty, intoned the Black people.

Imagine if you can, the entire population of Jamaica
can be accommodated on Rhode Island; and my first
white Christmas spent alone in a Queen's apartment.

Here is a secret I learned from experience: there is
a finite number of times that one can descend into
a New York subway. Should you exceed or overstep
your ride-quota, the New Lots train will station itself
in your head. To be rid of its iron-squat, you must
get brain washes in warm Caribbean sea water, or
you'll sit by Grand Central station and weep, or fall
off at Brooklyn's last exit. I confess: I looked behind
as I left, the wide sky over the Hudson was burning.

I Buy My Son a Reed

All day, John Coltrane invoking a Love Supreme,
woke up with him. In the slumber days before
the why of the reed's insistence shook me

I'd play H. Mann's Battle Hymn, soft beginning,
Shams of Tabriz asking Rumi sly trick questions,
near the end all the entire reed bed is keening.

I buy my son a reed instrument, for Shams,
in thanks for the days I woke in charnel house
unconscious, yet here I am, relating this tale.

He does not touch the reed, wanting to postpone
the must and bound day when said instrument
will function as straight extension of his breath.

Let's say now he will not. Leave it, I too slept late.
Today here's John Coltrane, who desired to become
a saint; his giant steps shook down sheets of sound

to wrap and seal off heart's core. I was twelve
when I heard someone say his lungs contained
air enough to move large rooms. May my son's.

I Saw Charles Mingus

There went Mingus, high as he was wide,
moving stately galleon up fifth avenue.
Tall valkyrie-blonde woman heartside,
they changed sides, crossed over
on approaching the New School. It was cold.
How did I see Charles Mingus pass?
I cashiered at Rugoff's Fifth Avenue
between Twelfth and Thirteenth Street
after classes at the Art Students League.
One extra A train token busted my budget.
But you don't want to hear that; to you
I'm an island upstart, allowed in through
tradesperson's entrance. True that, but
point is I did see Mingus, walking. As I
cashiered, Master Akira Kurosawa reeled.

A Simple Apology

The old woman marks time; her hoarse voice
fans into white plumes, she asks Anna Akhmatova
standing as one in a long cold line of suffering,
"Can you describe this?" And Anna (half nun
half whore Stalin called her) says "yes."

Come Anna:

Lest we all become like Job
and lay hands over our mouths.

How the neo-surrealists flee
to fantastical graveyards
of Louisiana. Under amber
Bayou moon, they scan tomb
language. Invoke Marie la Veau,
New Orleans' medicine woman,
to conjure them fit description.

Language poets enter: utter
strict forged grammar codes
you cannot break. Let them speak,
let them speak.
You cannot wait; wash your words
till Anna comes.
Simple soap of Walt Whitman or
a good Jamaican.

Just say sincerely,

I am sorry for your loss.

LORNA GOODISON is an associate professor of English at the University of Michigan. Her previous books include *Selected Poems* (1992), *To Us, All Flowers Are Roses* (1995), *Turn Thanks* (1999), and *Travelling Mercies* (2001). She was born and raised in Jamaica.

Illinois Poetry Series
Laurence Lieberman, Editor

Dear John, Dear Coltrane
Michael S. Harper (1985)

Poems from the Sangamon
John Knoepfle (1985)

In It
Stephen Berg (1986)

The Ghosts of Who We Were
Phyllis Thompson (1986)

Moon in a Mason Jar
Robert Wrigley (1986)

Lower-Class Heresy
T. R. Hummer (1987)

Poems: New and Selected
Frederick Morgan (1987)

Furnace Harbor: A Rhapsody of the
    North Country
Philip D. Church (1988)

Bad Girl, with Hawk
Nance Van Winckel (1988)

Blue Tango
Michael Van Walleghen (1989)

Eden
Dennis Schmitz (1989)

Waiting for Poppa at the Smithtown
    Diner
Peter Serchuk (1990)

Great Blue
Brendan Galvin (1990)

What My Father Believed
Robert Wrigley (1991)

Something Grazes Our Hair
S. J. Marks (1991)

Walking the Blind Dog
G. E. Murray (1992)

The Sawdust War
Jim Barnes (1992)

The God of Indeterminacy
Sandra McPherson (1993)

Off-Season at the Edge of the World
Debora Greger (1994)

Counting the Black Angels
Len Roberts (1994)

Oblivion
Stephen Berg (1995)

To Us, All Flowers Are Roses
Lorna Goodison (1995)

Honorable Amendments
Michael S. Harper (1995)

Points of Departure
Miller Williams (1995)

Dance Script with Electric Ballerina
Alice Fulton (reissue, 1996)

To the Bone: New and Selected Poems
Sydney Lea (1996)

Floating on Solitude
Dave Smith (3-volume reissue, 1996)

Bruised Paradise
Kevin Stein (1996)

Walt Whitman Bathing
David Wagoner (1996)

Rough Cut
Thomas Swiss (1997)

Paris
Jim Barnes (1997)

National Poetry Series

Cities in Motion
Sylvia Moss (1987)
Selected by Derek Walcott

The Hand of God and a Few Bright
    Flowers
William Olsen (1988)
Selected by David Wagoner

The Great Bird of Love
Paul Zimmer (1989)
Selected by William Stafford

Stubborn
Roland Flint (1990)
Selected by Dave Smith

The Surface
Laura Mullen (1991)
Selected by C. K. Williams

The Dig
Lynn Emanuel (1992)
Selected by Gerald Stern

My Alexandria
Mark Doty (1993)
Selected by Philip Levine

The High Road to Taos
Martin Edmunds (1994)
Selected by Donald Hall

Theater of Animals
Samn Stockwell (1995)
Selected by Louise Glück

The Broken World
Marcus Cafagña (1996)
Selected by Yusef Komunyakaa

Nine Skies
A. V. Christie (1997)
Selected by Sandra McPherson

Lost Wax
Heather Ramsdell (1998)
Selected by James Tate

So Often the Pitcher Goes to Water
    until It Breaks
Rigoberto González (1999)
Selected by Ai

Renunciation
Corey Marks (2000)
Selected by Philip Levine

Manderley
Rebecca Wolff (2001)
Selected by Robert Pinsky

Theory of Devolution
David Groff (2002)
Selected by Mark Doty

Rhythm and Booze
Julie Kane (2003)
Selected by Maxine Kumin

Shiva's Drum
Stephen Cramer (2004)
Selected by Grace Schulman

Other Poetry Volumes

Local Men and *Domains*
James Whitehead (1987)

Her Soul beneath the Bone: Women's
    Poetry on Breast Cancer
Edited by Leatrice Lifshitz (1988)

The University of Illinois Press
is a founding member of the
Association of American University Presses.

University of Illinois Press
1325 South Oak Street
Champaign, IL 61820-6903
www.press.uillinois.edu